ONEMENT WON

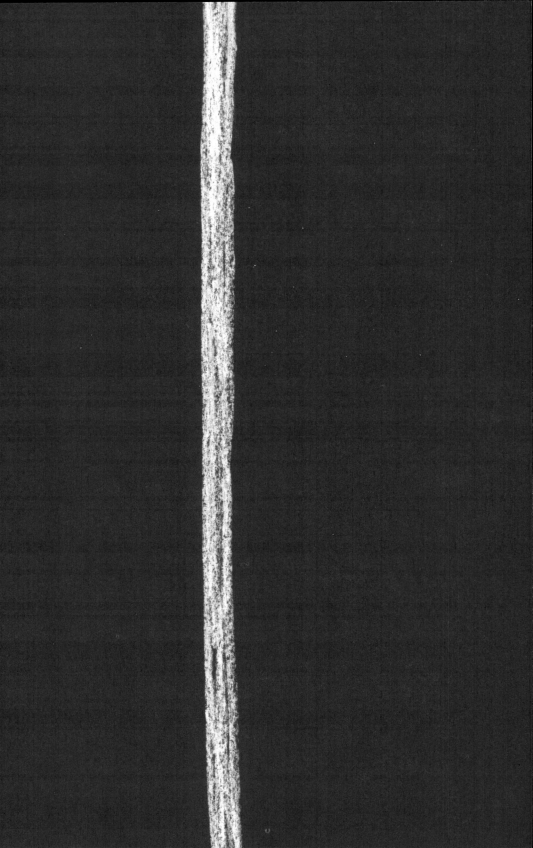

PRAGEETA SHARMA

Onement Won

WAVE BOOKS SEATTLE / NEW YORK

Published by Wave Books

www.wavepoetry.com

Copyright © 2025 by Prageeta Sharma

All rights reserved

Wave Books titles are distributed to the trade by

Consortium Book Sales and Distribution

Phone: 800-283-3572 / SAN 631-760X

Library of Congress Cataloging-in-Publication Data

Names: Sharma, Prageeta, author.

Title: Onement won / Prageeta Sharma.

Description: First edition. | Seattle : Wave Books, 2025.

Series: Wave Books ; 125

Identifiers: LCCN 2025008166 | ISBN 9798891060357 (paperback)

Subjects: LCGFT: Poetry.

Classification: LCC PS3619.H35664 O54 2025 | DDC 811/.6—dc23/eng/20250404

LC record available at https://lccn.loc.gov/2025008166

Designed by Crisis

Printed in the United States of America

9 8 7 6 5 4 3 2 1

First Edition

Wave Books 125

For my beloved mother and husband

BIMLA SHARMA

(1942–2023)

MICHAEL STUSSY

(1958–2023)

Irresistible Contentment

1

Secular Ornament

2

A Memory of Its Ceasing

3

Metaphorically Charged

6

Inside the Sunlight of Lost Friendship, Squint So You Can See Yourself Again

8

A Legacy

10

A One Won

12

Sunday, Sunday

14

Lateral Violence

15

A Moment Has Two Equal Parts and Many Decades

17

Art Is the Device to Get Out of Despair

24

Love, Death, and Shadows (1959) *in Missoula*

26

Ornament

28

What Is Sovereignty for the Hindu Today?

30

Thinking Through Supremacy in Hinduism

31

"One of the Strongest Fears Is the Fear of the Unknown"

32

How a Tale Lost Its Ending

34

Hostilities That Are Not Hostilities

36

The Imperishable and Perishable Family

37

This Day

38

Philip Glass

39

Friendment

40

Elegance and Rights

42

Widowing

44

Envy and Gratitude

46

Animal Family

48

Mothering

50

Maternal Endings

56

Moment #1

58

Onement

60

Value in Failure

62

Long-Term Intimacy and Terminal Illness

64

The Restoration

65

Living Room

67

You, a Graceful Place

69

Keeping Still

70

I Am Learning to Find the Horizons of Peace

72

Vir Heroicus Sublimis

74

Passions of the Void

75

Abstract Expressionist

76

Index

81

Acknowledgments

85

How do I live without Hari? How, mother?

—Mirabai, "Mira Loses It"

ONEMENT WON

Irresistible Contentment

I am talking my way back to the poem's turn
and where it might lie outside my skirted body,
a corded place where bluish sky paints my attention,
and empties itself into a golden silence—
without talk or sound. Phrases now feel
perversely sentient and yet devilishly
wrong. Every night I talk with the hope
that speech itself will burn me
its one true alphabet.
Nevertheless, morning's magic
always looks opaque because
a stronger feeling replaced
the lesser one, and the rightness
must reach the poem's hearted center
so that I am led to what might be
a plateau of nested changes, something
irresistible, those letters of gold, maybe anew.

Secular Ornament

This is an ornament for the mind, a support for the mind.
—Dana Sutta: Giving

Throughout this fallen fall into a diminished winter

with its ten thousand upturned leaves,
its impervious starlight for which I was given sight to look up, Upa,
having perceived the mind,
in an imperceptible

snowed-in shadow. A demarcated yellow.

I was given a future to breathe in.

I am still discussing what traumas won't shake.

Could they lessen in time?

Why do you think I am with him because he is at peace with himself
and brings his peace to me.

There is incalculable value in the quiet night of nonviolent affairs.

A Memory of Its Ceasing

The memory we have in us of a time before physical time is the memory of this end: our memory of utter soul-being, possessed through the body's witness to what-has-occurred, is a memory of its ceasing.
—Laura Riding Jackson, *The Telling*

I grew up in an old shamble house now overbuilt, decorative for several decades,
but now with a slight gangly tarnish of neglect.

It's still full of Hindu and Christian idols and celebrities:
Swami Ramakrishna, Sai Baba, and Jesus Christ.

The idols still sit with and without purpose, as officers, relics,
and spiritual registers.

I find I am now freely espousing but also finding these marks
of idolatry in poetry.

And so, this is about coming back to a normalized moment with a steep,
and yet numbered center: one that does not grouse at bitter states,
not in the hot room of hibernated troubles.

This is the one about when consciousness *becomes* exciting,
or about developing a feeling of benevolence towards a meager process.

This is about loving what is ordinary and its sentient onement,
        about loving a slow drain that drowns the enormity
with oneself and the localized system of numbering my thumbs.

This is about finding all the freighted blankets and figuring out
that the itchy pain returns in syntactical tatters.

It's about earning a kind of uninhibited hurting
and finding that it is not an unfathomable creed without a lesson.

It is about the "I" that does the choosing of memories for a truer vision—
in seeing what might be down the vituperative road
and freeing this vision from its shame.

What kind of people are down the road for me?

Who sees me in kindness? Who do I see back in kindness?

I have tried to leave some coldness in the carrels behind,
in search for a new library desk.

This is about human consciousness, personality, and the abstract scripture I might
try to induce.

But there is loss.

I am losing my mother who taught me that Hinduism has ethics in love
and friendship, even when she has been coarse about all of it.

(4)

I, too, have been coarse: and thus lost meaningless friends

for which only I am weighted down in bouts of sadness . . .

but to free it from pages, from falsities, how spacious.

This is about coming back to oneself.

No Ram Dass. No Be Here Now.

No Om of sitting in place.

This is about size and succumbing.

Metaphorically Charged

I meant well and resisted comparisons
for a while because those who might cajole
me into finding their inaccuracy accurate
need likenesses. I was meant to find myself inside a metaphor
but I wasn't there and felt disillusioned.
Instead I built the word with the bricks of what comparison
might mean with another suffix,
what I meant was I was keen to add nouns.
I wanted to add "wound" to the comparison
and build its condition to be matter-of-fact.

I found the condition of the wound
to be built into its state of cruelty.
She said they have wounds too, and that's why they feel
this way. I said, I'm not trying to wound them
but they like thinking of my wounds in a certain way.

I find their wounds to effect cruelty
and mine did not intend the same effect.

I'm angry at those who've been economical about what I might
have meant. I'm despairing because I created meaning
from a grievance nobody dared to own.

They wanted to possess the grievance after it was vetted,

and I didn't want to give it to them.

So they lied about what

they thought of comparisons which

are metaphors lying about what they said they mean.

Inside the Sunlight of Lost Friendship, Squint So You Can See Yourself Again

My soul entire, is that animal rasp.

—Goethe, *Faust*

Maybe there's a white stripe-light of sentience in view, just as
my barking goldendoodle perches her head on the sofa's arm to yawn
a longing into the carpet. We are held inside a tepid sunlight,
warming the desultory day with body heat and blankets.
Even in California, it chills. No other humans are here today.
Mike is at the cancer hospital
and I am inside my corner ruminating the end of a friendship.
(It functions as a distraction or a way to self-loathe
something more tangible than processing the fears inside.)
I thought this friendship was solid.
I'm embarrassed to be seen so pusillanimously by her.
(I am something ugly, with both rage and timidity,
and that combination bothers people.)
Especially now, when things are harder than I imagined.
She thought I was still her old needy friend, like
when Dale died, and she made an effort then to show me she cared.
I held onto it dearly. I think people who haven't lost a partner or spouse
don't understand what their gestures might mean. And now she seems
out of sorts, distraught, mean, like-not-herself. Things happened

to her that she wouldn't share with me.

I badgered her to tell me what I did wrong or what wrong

had happened between us, or changed these last few years,

and she refused. She stayed withdrawn, a move I've seen too much.

Then she gaslighted, another move of too much and no more.

Only the truth for me now. Ultimately, she gave me excuses, and I became *the problem.*

I kept trying to figure out what I did. She wouldn't admit she had hostility but was hostile

and denied it, which was even more aggressive.

Have I expected too much from friends?

And yet, dear ones give me a broad spectrum of love.

Why do I settle into gray affliction like it's my new living room?

What ossifying conditions change friends into enemies?

It's a habit of fervor that I need to end now.

I will tell myself that I'm happy without her,

and I've been without her for a long time,

and changed, but this habit is trailing me

with its dissolution, in its sad bankruptcy without sunlight,

just like all capitalist feelings that sing along vacancies.

What is the meaning of loneliness anyway? Is it what invariably

accompanies these shadows, these investments? I bother myself

by making so much confession,

as Mike journeys along to infusion land. And this ruminating

is not fair to him. But I wanted the poem to be honest about

its pathologies, its self-talk, and what the work of suffering-thoughts do.

And yet I realize, very slowly, which he would appreciate,

that I arrived somewhere, to a truer belief from all

the aching sorrow: sometimes it's not the people you miss.

It's the longing you had to be understood by them.

A Legacy

All this noisy commotion isolated a fairly
small universe of nothing special.
I faced the assistant to the incumbent,
his failed face of poetry bottomless
with self-pride and a satisfaction that fed his wolf.
And he was a wolf
and when I scoffed at him
with some penetration I could see the clamor
of his wounds and also the vanity
in his recognitions. He believed it his right
to judge me and thought I was undeserving
and his judgment, a stun gun, took
my gender and race and euthanized
its center, and he thought this
was an extension of the occult,
that it was the intuition
of a bright star
affecting forward.
I wanted him to see this in a particular
light but the particular worsened into
a bruise of matter far more inhumane,
and I fell into its hole and he, with his glee,
had no idea, because his gender and race
gave him the privilege to look down

and see how my skeleton warped my will
but not the firmament of my broadness,
and what I know now as measuring across
power and enduring many luminary deficits
that come out of symptoms and their fallen edges.

A One Won

In it I found that the political discourse would love its ethical moon.

A wonderment. A one sum.

Bewitching affinities built upon antinomies. Abstract: an expression, a wool cap
of ornament for the sake of weather.

Loving him helplessly anew helped. Loving her helplessly anew helped.

Leaving it all behind helplessly helped.

Building around the moribund became a kind of blessing.

              I left constituents around the number one and I won,
           and I felt simple and glad,

and finally, incandescent, and comfortably large in my honesty:
a kind of hanging of the rituals,
the clothes, the sense of living in them upright.

            I felt trouble pinging from my thumb muscles but ignored the throb.

I looked out and out into a dense and driven fog and said goodbye to its flavor.

Goodbye to more than ten years of saying *Will you please love me?*

I wanted to birth a kind of abstract expressionism of the merely objective
and the racialized lover of things.

Onement or ornament or I won an ornament or I loved an ornament
and the onement of myself resolved.

I resolved and thus I became into myself a one

that I thought would never be allowed.

I moved outside of the fog into a place that signified art.

Sunday, Sunday

A Katha December I see in the looming white of morning.

I want to feel more sentient, I say to the blankets and to the neurological
labor I hope to integrate.

I don't want the ingestible lyric of my body to blindfold me.
I do wonder what David Lynch has learned from the Upanishads.

I found this translation too summarizing, too commercial.
I want to go to the other one, full of repetition and of "That which is that,"
or this, or about intention and spirit.

What words are set to become the Supreme Self in the making?
That which is a supreme Sunday turning into a Monday.
Why is "supreme" set up to mediate value?

Lateral Violence

FOR VALORIE

First a flabby belittlement by some well-meaning
white folks when they cross me because they weren't meaning
to, they say. It was only that I had become wholly invisible
and they enjoy their heaping, entitled vocalizations
that enforce their platforms of corporeal speech.

But through this I learned that I had no real power to wield,
and this crown I wore, glittering in green fermentation,
put my head into a state of chronic query.
My desire is lost in a fomenting chrome.

But then I noticed my solidarity sisters sniff out my lack, too,
and the vascular trauma of hurt in my blood became
a wound in my innermost molecules.

Distinctions around difference and assimilation fester
and hurt feelings erupt from lateral power.
It pains much worse because they seem to be playing
out a supremacy of whiteness, of wielding power
from which an outspread lack peels away to a nothingness
marked with the pinkest cardinal feelings.

I don't believe we outright demean each other,
we might just be trying to fit ourselves in,
hating all the spirals inside of the shape
trying to let them fizz or spark, but a wrongness
emerges replacing the earned principled feeling.

I say all this because I look back on how power systems
at play in microaggressions still impart feelings
of terror because they annihilate, desecrating
the inner self-protection one might seed or learned behind
some favored sanguine curtains.

I recall myself there hiding a judgment going back colonial centuries:
how it sticks in fenced edges. How I knew trying to make friends
would undo my best intentions and thwart so much
of what had been a fernery of deep and culminating sympathies.
My heart, my mind, my head hoped we'd have real intimacy—
bonded connections based on our chunky hardships,
not the hard bitten loss in the over-harvested field of
scarcity knocking several of us down with full force.
And now do we sit in this field, doing the scholarly work
of facing the empire, but wounded from those
whom we bitterly wanted on our side, not on our back.

A Moment Has Two Equal Parts
and Many Decades

Relationships of power are never fully suspended, even as the occult appears to banish
the distinctions that dissident Anglo-Indians so disdained in the colonial administration.
—Viswanathan 2000, 3–4

Cartesian voiceovers may draw you in by your desire for authenticity,
but there are people, esoterics, who want to buy you a soul
in how they narrate a life, pencil in hand.

Theosophists, too. What they espouse in the occult is Orientalism.
It travels to the current day, to our current soul-making.

I say, *they don't care about you.*
I thought they did. I thought they might.

Many like them—in new iterations—
read Ram Dass and reconsidered politics but grew too tired of how
one must try to be in this world. And failed to consider the drawn-in hierarchies.

To heal I found cultural influences to be symbols,
and myself in between in my head of longing to identify.

Let it be, say Lennon and McCartney.

McCartney, a widower

Lennon widowed a genius, an intelligent and scrappy Japanese American woman.

Along with this, Olivia Harrison, widowed by her sadhu-loving husband.

Along with Barnett Newman's zip across my face

dividing my sense of division of what inhabits my world.

The pain of strong men making art. Their pain clutched in their grips

and in their sides, and how they hurled me into their hell, but I loved their minds.

I found both abstraction and pain, in art, in the Beatles and in the museum.

I waited so eagerly for that line's other shoe to drop,

but I have to wake up and live.

I must take distance from everyone else's paintings, from their lives

and lies, and see a moment clearly: as a memory having two equal parts.

I can't be anyone but myself nor can I hold my arms

still the way some can in action.

I hope to see luck in the moment it appears,

      as it might shine,

in the line, a zip, down the middle of a canvas,

or as an intermediary posing gladly in a piercing photograph

that others might first see as dull.

Lennon found love in a gallery. I find love in a gallery, over and over and over.

I don't know if the Beatles actively cited the Upanishads but were inspired by
the Bhagavad Gita, and Geeta means song,

and my name means preface to a song, which song? Is it a spiritual song?

Did I lose it along the way?

Did I find I needed a spiritual center from the populist world?
The one that remade my culture?

The one that made me rename myself as an adolescent to approximate my name?

When I was a teenager I wanted people to call me Angel or *Anjali* so I had an Indian-
sounding name that could be converted to a sultry American name. It was my first poem,
my first lyric.

This helped me disassociate from the name-calling and bullying in middle
and high school because they had turned my name into a slur and taunted me with it.

I had to reimagine another name that went with my heavy metal eyeliner,

my love of Aerosmith which then turned
to Ono's "Yes, I'm your Angel," living in both of those song-feelings,
when the moment came to utter a legible name.

I realize I don't want to live with anyone's dry-off tone, a slow-moving hostility:
undetectable at first but then shapes to a simper
absent of remorse, sadness, or probity—

discounting how these conditions might teach
when punctuated in volvelles.

And now, as an adult, when my fellow friends lose solidarity with one another
and then they commit lateral violence, especially
when they can't name what they do with power.

This is what is happening to our unity as a global people.

The fallen sun, the rising moon, its discs in measurement.
This medieval purpose of finding daylight burning
is to locate a concrete metaphor amidst
snow-covered vowels—that patchwork of a social life here.

I am not calling out solely in a lyric utterance,
because how when narrated with small and smaller talk,
it's almost extinguishing, damaging the selves underneath—
the striking timidity of a companion ungrasping hands
to let the air cool and let sweat dissolve.

*   *   *

I saw you all at the important table and surmised that
I did know all of you in singularity or with trust.

I take this memory of you to the other self,
here to this new collaborative, to a new idea of onement.

(20)

I recommend finding reality honest, and the sewing materials rip open
to a flighted fault line of straight upright branches,
how you drive away from them to the state line.
This is the old life sewn into the new one, and it doesn't have

to be excitable all the time.

I recommend looking into the expressive expression
of your blushing brown cheek in the window's reflection—
to find that innermost feeling with its failed circuitry,
because now you are becoming content with contentedness

in what is mine or yours to win because winning is how won
stays won; as it feels in its innermost present-sense and matches a bronze tree
outside your new house and its silver windows.

How foisted and difficult the cabaret of showmanship is to watch—
leather-tight clothes around the girth, performing a lighted clarification
that hurts in retrospect but its honesty is beguiling
and it touched you, me, and this moment.

I have brought my heart-lit candles with their figurative cascades.

And I give it to whom, my neighbor?

Or to this overgenerous darling quipped in his comely quiet-dance,
the one we don't do in public.

Because a nightly living room for a nightly night of proportions will fulfill more of my fantasy than dining with the scholar's mouth.

Or how the address and the idea of numeracy in life, in repetition, becomes memorable and not numerous because you understand death now, and for the rest of your life,

you will always find death—in plain terms—in your headspace.

But what I collect for my oldest Hindu self is one held out in ancestry and for lineage and for prosperity like three cultural questions singe a need or purpose.

So with blushing, I am letting my arms lower in obedience. I have obedience to my parents and I hunger this.

I have hunger for an eternal partner. And you are here.

I hunger this more than poetry. This is the cultural expression I won't let up.

But I am in admiration of what being numerous means in modernism
        and its ethos. I am still wanting an occult that can be measured

with atheist overtures particularly when I feel moved by you.

This is also coupled with a yearning to exit into and out of the communal

through numbering the stairwells with the small hand I have been given
        that has grown significant, but burned out.

Tired out by triggers that bore pupils above pupils. I wanted to eat my own populism and cry *forgive me*.

I handed you a jackfruit that we all found teeming and built.

I thought this was a part of Atman.

The spiritual subjectivity of the soul but in use in other words, as if I found their multiple speakers inside of connoisseurship.

A fortune without a karmic narrative and yet imbuing karma's light
with a touch, a nod, a feeling that avows something.

A chin piqued to say *yes* and *of course.*

Let all the lines be as they must, both ornamental and necessary,

and leaven our hearts to be both representational and nonrepresentational.

Art Is the Device to Get Out of Despair

After Reading Sandra Soto's "Feel Lags (for José)"

Release me into this world we made together for a moment
but then get me into the poem quickly before more hurting arises.
I am thinking about how I can't cure your cancer or extend our time together
beyond what fate allows. Each day we fight nausea, fatigue, or bowel discomforts.
All impede on your strength. I try to slide each worry into a revision,
in the poem, but no revision constitutes remission, nor NED, or an operable option.
Can I get you well enough for every existential decision we face?

We sometimes sob into the cool evenings as we hold
ourselves open to what-comes-next. I thought I left a calibrating world in its dome,
several years ago, but it followed us here to California. And yet, it is here that we have held
a time that "hangs back," a sun that quietly cajoles, a way to let grief become
    "straightforward."

I thought your health secure but this was an ableist wish we able-bodied have,
until one of us isn't anymore. Now we need to lift clarity up high to prosper—
this new knowledge's potency is harsh and bright blue, and my pains have
curled inward alongside my hands and joints.
How do I find a way to let art console me as I step

sideways into a fallen destination? Every morning I wake
to a bigger crack that might potentially swallow our mobilizing for survivorship and turn
    it into

a dust to spackle the unbeing, the *dull awareness* I often held in Sandy's essay on Muñoz
and how we gathered in solidarity with the hummingbirds
of April nesting us in pink sugar water. Katie reminds me how much community
Sandy and Raquel create and it is true. I know this and how I read it in their pages.

Love, Death, and *Shadows* (1959) in Missoula

FOR SEAN HILL

All errant glances looking off-frame or directly at you audience in unresolved fury.
I teach in our concave classroom, with its ascending wooden, hard-backed chairs,
and our flimsy broken shade with a stuck pull-cord. Crimson-light glares the room
so we squint to watch. I stand at a too-large podium in a haunted building.

I've been told some ghost stories and I've been known to share radical
ideas that were experienced as uncomfortable. Leslie Fiedler
may have been in the same room,
reconstructing the *Eros and Thanatos*, the interracial love, he foregrounded
in essays. *The antimarriage: freeing the protagonists of classic*
   American fiction from the adult entanglements of heterosexual passion, marriage, and
      domestic obligations . . .
And he is writing in the 1950s and *Shadows* shot in New York
where Fiedler's publisher lives, but Fiedler is here for some of the decade, in *his* English
   department understanding the racial conflicts and homoeroticism
before he writes *No! in Thunder*. After *Shadows* we talk about the racial hierarchy of
the characters and the theme of passing; what about hypodescent and, here,
what do we make of blood quantum, too.
And we haven't gotten to the heteronormative
   white culture of the literary scene at the highbrow party.
And Lelia Goldoni feels she can be Lelia and we are not certain if she can or not.
What kind of identification can she really have, or is it character immersion?

Who among us in this classroom is African American? Nobody.
We finish the conversation about improvisation acting and "natural feelings."
We agree how much we like Charles Mingus and Shafi Hadi.
We talk about poetics and code-switching and there is an elated sense of
connection I start to feel. I want them to know that the heap of film on Cassavetes's
floor was the poem representing his unknowable reach and he was going
to have to take on its contradictions without knowing 21st-century critical race
theory and let his characters talk through their ideas, assertions, and pain.
The interruptions on screen: characters' eyebrows, their compositional faces studied,
their acting & finish of a film that, in its early disappearance, its second version, screened
   with *Pull My Daisy* still gave its transitions their moving edges and let Benny
And Lelia and Hugh, as Caylin said in class, give us a cohesive family;
their tenderness anchors so much integration during segregation.
      And it was here with Fiedler coming back to his raft
and leaving the buffaloes of Montana for Buffalo, New York.
A place where poets found poetics in the future somehow;
     why are the themes of miscegenation haunting us here? or befuddling?
     We have poets too. Are we still resisting remote adorations & narativity's
     formula for what couldn't be said about love and death in 1959
     and what still can't be said now? Must it be through the improvisation that we find
     the substance and look at its ghost-sightings and who wrote or shot film of whom?
    and why?
      And why do I stand here feeling like it's all so hard to hold on to?

Ornament

FOR JOYCE LU

Let us substitute ornament for flesh as the germinal matter for making of the racialized gender.
—Anne Anlin Cheng

The 2nd type: is abstract. This means that the painting is of objects, but they have been reduced
to just the essentials, and, there are as many ways to do this as there are people doing it.
—Frederick Hammersley from "Something concrete on the abstract" talk

There is a lived experience in what description marks, what it paints, even in the stroke
    resisting
symbols or objects or ornaments, and yet retain its sense of being, even as it restates
    what in being
is lived in or "up with in," as within is painted or in making.

I say this to myself when I'm *up with in* the feeling. Does it feel like it's completed?
Does the thingness I symbolize do a better job of describing?

I see a circle as being coerced into its inference, into its tangle of carbons and peach,
of whittled green finding points and thus becoming an essentialist.

I have, of late, renounced purity in my culture's religious rhetoric
and so I won't find paintings of pure color clarifying.
I will not locate a hierarchical center; it collects its objects like ornaments.

(28)

But can I explain to you how easy it is for me to project myself into the painting?
Just as if it were my reality, my solace, myself colorizing as a feature of agency
into the whiteness of a canvas.

Abstraction becomes a way of featuring a sense of reality,
and ornamentation or an ornament I borrowed from Newman's *Onement*,
but now ascribing a space to a new painting, or to a world Anne Cheng discusses
as a self in ornamentalism, restating "with in" to a color-noun beyond a symbol.

What Is Sovereignty for the Hindu Today?

The self in Hindu thought, even in the individual, is a synonym for the Universal.
—Bipin Chandra Pal

What is universal now but a hierarchy? In that it still develops too much consensus around its power. What is the reprise of colonial Hinduism with so much of the self? How do we take up space in place? How did this all become the New Age? Where is the self here in Southern California where we have erased the communities with our settling universal selves? Is it the universal that keeps people out? What is a self in Hindu thought? Who is myself in Hindu thought, and what is mystic about this? What is the reprise of the individual who is a synonym of the self? Maybe the power of Shakti can be the new synonym, with its sense of "to be able." But is the problem of being able also a caste-privilege mentality? And is this still reining in the institution of the self. Why then do we build such assemblage around it as ritual but not check in to what might be too self-determined.

Thinking Through Supremacy in Hinduism

Remove the burning feeling in my brain,
rooting through flaws, ordeals, and avowals,
and missing the point of what my culture can be versus what it is.

Dangerous incantations espouse
social scale based on registered purity.
Ancient branding of surnames colorize status
and markings. All the Brahman trappings.

I see waving orange voltage watts
assuaged in chances that might signify hierarchies.
The body can be calmed, pleased, even, by any repetitious
chant. Rural violence: women and bodies are weaponized in shame.
This atrocity by Hindus in the name of piety and namesakes.
Rape and death sanctioned, uses of sati practiced.

Gandhi processed shared experiences of discrimination
when he was led by the neck to disturbances,
developed a puritanical stance and missed
the symbolism baked into it.
Prime ministers promote along the lines of what we have seen in the United States.
Right-wing rhetoric, supremacy of religion over vulnerable bodies.
I am tired of the terms that forfeit comprehension
and place laboring determinacy into structures of dominion.

"One of the Strongest Fears
Is the Fear of the Unknown"

(after Krishnamurti)

We are on our way to Seattle to enjoy the verdant landscape you love
and so that you may be treated by a new oncologist.

I had been fretting about the trip but it's really a fear of an indescribable future.
One that I can't paint in terms of scenery or markers.

Yet in this following of fear around too many corners,
which as Krishnamurti says about fear:
"We are apt to make an abstraction of fear,
that is to make an idea of fear. But we never listen, apparently
to the voice of fear that is telling its story."

So I will listen to its voice: I will listen during our long drive with two animals
curled in the backseat, one in a small crate, the other finally trying to nurture her.
The dog noses the cat with a sweetness.

I will pay attention to their sighs and voices.
I will take in images of the road's character as it drowns in a brown plain.

We forgot your camera and will have to rely
upon our phones to document the cool air-conditioned feeling
against the hot exterior of roads and the portraits we discover.

I must notice the days are precious and roads are scant with cars.
A solace of steady days. Do not sink to the fear of unknowns.

I must think like Rilke, be only isolated in thought, in
writing. Look up. Take in the sensorial, even in stink.

Evaluate the world right now: There is a chemical smell followed by dung
scenting the car from the fields. The knowns are these bright mountains
and an easy highway, the knowns can be insistent as odors.

Our worries are for the cows who look uncomfortably crowded.
Not for the free rein we believed in because it makes us all feel sad and packaged.

Look today at fear as an abstraction. It is an idea of the road, not murky,
not the "actual state of fear" as it will only be introspective.

You are staying in the complex abject that takes you into
moments that are too frightened, too enclosed,

to understand that all "consciousness is partial."

How a Tale Lost Its Ending

Sometimes I blame the years that came before and the girth on giving everyone everything.
I gave nothing to myself except food, wine, sugar, and hunger.

I was keen to be loved by a family who wasn't really mine, in the end, I realize.
My parents loved worrying about my weight and so they didn't feel like

the family I chose. My husband and his child pretended I wasn't bigger
each year, surrounding me for fifteen years as I grew fat in their care.

But then I learned, after he died, how little in common we all had except for food,
and the extravagance of a fevered materialism, of drinking nights away.

What could shape the heft of a dinner table isolating its troubles?

My weight hid all their vices and secrets. I was an overweighted fairy tale.

I didn't know what was tied to my neck. Was I full of myself?

Yes. Now, I am full of only myself.

It wasn't their fault or mine, necessarily, and maybe it was me who envied them?
Their weight, looks, and secrecies untouched, pathologies, however, welted into

our daily life and I became their central psychological problem because everything
stayed in a befuddling superficiality to me, of magical thinking where nothing burst

(34)

of consequence, unless in a private abuse. No discarding that calculated vanity
because a privilege is a decidedly discovered specious affair for some.

But oh they loved my Ganesh and Krishna, all the Gopal babies!
Oh they loved my Hinduism for what it gave them—launching a misdirected

spiciness. I was able to mount their greed with judicious garlands. And maybe my blue
roundness held their sanctity entwined until a burst. I burst with anger.

I, myself, was my culture, and for them, used for their yogic poses,
and when they wore Indian textiles around their middles,

and draped a mantra with a vowel around their tongues for fitness.

How much mimicry built a thrusting shell, and how when I succumbed to their values

I felt like a thin, cheap version of myself.

Spreading butter on top of a fake family until they felt suffocated by my headlong will,
and they robbed my big Buddha belly of what I hoped were my good deeds.

Hostilities That Are Not Hostilities

I see the force of a celebrant with power in gold banglettes
on somebody's hilltop. I was reminded of my mother while admiring it,

as she loves miscible jewelry all over hands and wrists. I thought one moment garish,
even as I was raised in this quality and felt it a real acquisition. I was cut

from my mother's cloth because I agreed wholeheartedly in how I couldn't help my own
tastelessness. I tried to admit it as a fault line but saw the contradiction

it held up in the light. It was my mother, an immigrant. She wanted me to blister about,
shoving my own power aside into the trees. I did but became

embarrassed when we all fell over, truncating our purposes, ridiculed, learning of a
recognition that I shouldn't have tried to build this particular push, especially in my

vulnerable state. I will never attach to power again and be put into the position of pleasing
a group to make my point. I called four of them bullies

because they misread my desires. I defended myself from their pettiness.
If they thought I was performing for them they are wrong. This is why celebrations can

sometimes end the day cheaply. Let's reassemble the discord, industrializing a brilliant cut,
the gem of bridging purposes burning the might of hostilities so their

prolonged pressure might truly break its thickset stench where we might find my mother
in bed nearing the end of her life. I must remember that it wasn't a worthless fight.

The Imperishable and Perishable Family

There was a husband-father at one time,
distinguished in phrases but not in gestures.
There was a daughter circulating in vain attempts, calculating the usage of efforts,
I'm afraid to say. I had painted her in pearly fabric
amidst the lost husband-father who blew up our foundation
when he sought to line draw the exaggerations in our field: what were perished
actions of the family. I thought to resuscitate it all and my cheeks blew inward.
I was holding all my breath inside. This wasn't a good idea.

So does this world spring from the imperishable, ask the Upanishads.

And led me to ask for a crystalline idiom, because in finding
the daughter, I lost myself. I realized (too late)
I was granted tyranny for all the lost occasions.
My therapist calls this manipulation. I decided to stake its claim.
I will be done now. I knew I was the hat trick for them.
And thus I'm over with the game because the game had since
been done with me—I had no idea until I blew and blew and blew.

This Day

I hear the coyotes howling behind this suburban house.

I want the couplets here to contain all the unplumbed melodrama
and strain of being in my hometown for these miserable days,

but the more I douse these stanzas with complaint,
the more I feel a calmness etch itself a tame,
casual care towards my singular family,
their private comforts,

the rodent mouse who hides in their walls, the pack of wilds
scrounge with me, in a feign of greed.

We all tire of getting old and weak,
and must share our house fears together, as we should.

Philip Glass

Snow dropping pellets
into the synthesizer.

I have curtains flattering
the window's flat tones.

I am in quiet reciprocity.

We used to hide out together
in friendship, and I felt so
enamored by your grace until I learned
that it was not a real gesture.

You were never my enemy until
I learned that I was yours
and that your perceptions
drew people away from you.
I believed in a certain fairness
and respect. It's not subjective,
but like Philip Glass I will learn
all there is about repetition
in art and life, how to see
crystallization in the syllables
of falling sounds.

Friendment

I would like to tell you how our friendship lost its appeal.

It was simple and petty, and was about the circumstances of power
and white feminism, how it simpers.

I saw how my symbol was porous in your pupil-eye
and I, your middle-class servant,

not real to you. You spoke ill of me.

It was shared with me and I fell sullen suddenly and bore my anger
till it fell into place with the categories I had for it.

I realized I was a kind of curtain to envisage with a sparring light
that shouldn't get in the way.

I was an outdated venetian blind with a cuckold cord
and not a long-standing mirror.
And I stopped believing your bright-eyed condemnation
of everyone across the widened and bolted table.

People who were decidedly likable. I knew they were.

There's a row of furniture that we all have to muscle,
and it hurts our arms and we are bruised now.

And without you we made dinner—with lobster bisque and strident chalices itemizing kindly
suggestions with holidays underneath the sentiment;
and it was overwhelmingly delightful.

And with this, we realize that arms give up holding the prideful
and turn to those with a bona fide devotion of humans.

Most of us are together in this project of leaving ambition
to some delightful happenstance and not construing people as prey.

But now I am the one who sounds superior. I want to retract some of this tone.

But I can't, I will say more to how I placed your authority above my head—a headless crown.

You find it necessary to reprove innocence
and I saw that squarely replace your radiance.

A poem, while it can expose us to our imagining selves, can also trick us into imagining
ourselves as something beyond our behaviors.

Elegance and Rights

How is it that I work so hard to find elegance and taste? How it might
only occupy other people's Sunday mornings, my blue silk, *of the peignoir.*

But the chiffon of Stevens, Pound, and Moore sticks. Maybe I inhaled it?
I sit in a replica Eames chair, and its simulated leather feels genuine to me.

I write a poem about the rose and yellow pillows, and those flowers

are not reproduced or stitched. The Orientalism I exist in is a different proliferation
and I must figure out, in my femininity, what is my subject?

I'm not committed to making a poem consume a pastoral joy or give birth.
Or adulate in my cultural heritage, or build a mimesis of its merits.

It may be something else: an interior self lashed or celebrated in between
the heart and the uterus, carefree to think about what the world might not bestow.

But governments seek to control our idea-of-purity, our bodies, our words,
our narratives. Governments and religion. They reproduce themselves. How to flee?

I can tell you that if the hummingbird came nearer I wouldn't shoo her away

with lyric nor would I give up the liberating moment when I could see how
I am finally comforted among the books, their selves, and the social decibel

of how I look into the outside; albeit, I'm still alienated by the legislation,
and how its rhetoric obliterates my rights, desires, and the domestic resilience

laundered in my tone. I will stay in the fabric of fibroin patterning,
my natural American scenery, cut out to the body of one using art

for therapy, for poetry, for life to please keep me loving the fiction of the self.

Widowing

The last of your studio boxes
towering this new basement that I clean for good. All this in
  year four.

In them I find a lone condom,
a buried treasure of your lost virility.

Was it saying something lonely to me?
And then not to me but to a stranger, another one?

When you were alive
I had found a condom in your computer bag.
You balked—in your stupid rage—
and told me it was so old—from when we used them, back in 2002.

I knew they only have a span of five years; they swim upstream in
      their packages.

This one expired in 2016. You died in 2015. When did you buy
      this last condom?

(Nobody talks about the difficult grieving process of mourning
      your husband and then his secrets and vices, left in corner
      plastic bins.)

But this is why I built a synthetic cave around my
        disappointments
like the chemicals that drowned your sense and reason
and left only an outward charm of deflection like a collected
        banality.

Your sister, a nurse, after washing your body,
cleaned up your fentanyl patches with their glassine
coverings on the laundry room floor, behind the washer and dryer.

You took it with your chemotherapy, but you were also sneaking
        it for years.

You were always searching for painkillers, hiding them high up
        from me.

Or in your bins, at your studio, full of drawings, cartoons, and
        scribbled poems

that make so obvious how you lived inside yourself with a kind
        of agony,

in your own fallible body, its chronic pain, and what it really
        called forth,
an insatiable carrying of a private penury, your only sojourn.

Envy and Gratitude

It feels like necessary witchcraft to hold these dueling emotions in my hands.
Gripping feelings like they're irreplaceable possessions even as several embarrass me
with their greed.

Some of the others give a final arriving solace.

Especially when they corrode like all hopeful technological devices, heating and spurning
into spinning globes then parachutes spiraling into the downward sea—a war of enabling
shoulders.

I then unleashed an endless amount of shame into my being like
the finishing feeling of the unnecessary screen time that hounds my biology.

I am shaken with the corruption they carry me into:

False regulations.

I want to lose this pride as fast as I can, a hot potato of uneven privilege, and the weird
gratitude

because it necessitates itself from the mishap of emotional impoverishment and stops
working its magic.

How does one unearth the other, is this a trash heap

of human folly? Do they both feel around for morality
and give me, in trepidation, humanity?

I can list five people who dislike me
and I envy just one of them.

I think they all disliked me

for the same issue that was meant to help lessen

envy and engender gratitude, to nurture solidarity
instead filled a soulless careerism.

In poetry and writing, no doubt.
I want to try and speak to the why of it

but I think it all lands in a soup of cruelty
and misgivings, and I don't envy

the mean streaks that graze the pond's surface,

for it is somewhat cloudy in the mirror
and the longish swamp

will hold your head down in its thickness.

Animal Family

There was a family of deer that looked something like us.
They traveled far with a fierce sense of collective unity.
Held their fearless faces absent of cosmic worry, for the most part.
And yet something crept in, making the easiest part
of being together a struggle. As fate would have it, they would eventually
have to make their way across several highways alone,
not in a pack of unity or disunity, but as singular beings.
The hardest part is some of them would die.
Some knew they might freeze in headlights
but survive. Some may creep across the Montana parks
without knowing who else might be lurking.
Others fell in love among the icicles of snow that dossal in sparkles.
Couples, we agree, are wintery mirages unto themselves.
This family, fragmented in a finitude of private loves,
hid in their respective emotional anxieties,
and separated their loyalties out as rations.
Because of it, they ventured out in their own ways,
finding snowberries in difficult spaces.
Acceding to those shrubs far out of reach.
This might have cost the family their comfort.
But it began the notion that every moon is an ornament
bobbing in front of a ghost light, and from which,
I used it to see, perceptually, that I am no more of that family.
To which, I found a solitary doe in a grove, an eyeful of meadow,

and a handful of buoyant well-wishers to take me
closer to a beckoning kinship, because it had been hidden
too much by the forest, too much by the obsolete family
who had taken my moonlight along with my wilderness.

Mothering

We are parents so that our children can be stepparents and their children can be childless.
—Michael Leong, "(Be)labored Posterities"

What can I say about Mother? We have not yet realized who she is.
—Svami Keshavananda and Kedarnath Datta

In the end I didn't have my own biological child.

I realize this was maybe the initial loss or a missing piece;

and being a mother is such a primary identity, all along,

I am told and it is reinforced.

I felt I was included in mothering as a stepmother
but learned how easy it is to let that person, the stepmother, go.

She's a tool, an aid, a manipulated appendage.

Cut her off.

I loved the idea that being a poet made up for this lack.

And yet, many people would ask, "When are you having a baby?"

Even my stepdaughter pursued this questioning as though
I would have a role if I provided her a sibling.

"When you and Dad have a baby, I'll raise it."

Her saying "I will raise it" felt greasy.

I am capable, just ambivalent. So I pulled that idea away, out of reach,
so I could stay inside my own desires.

Her father didn't want to have another child.

He thwarted pregnancy with insulting care, and guarded himself in many senses
from this question.

Why attach to one who isn't your own?

Why try to raise her? She has her own mother. Everyone said this to me.

They're never going to be yours. So why be a stepmother?

My own mother said, "blood is blood," but I didn't believe it at the time and I shook my
head No.

I revisited this after he died when I felt angst about whether she and I could still be a
family. I thought, when it's blood, you can almost disavow without realizing it.

I thought our family fluid, blended, fine in its formations,

but now understand that I must let go of power

in familial possession of the non-biological family.

But there is a draw. There is a punctuation to the effort.

Beleaguered by it, adding the ellipsis to my heart.

My emphasis.

There were signs I should have paid attention to,

but then I wouldn't get my present life, the subsequent

wideness of freedom I have now.

Winnicott's attachment is what I need to figure out.

And what have I done with Freud, did I let him go?

Even secular Hinduism has a hard time letting go of attachment.

We have to choose, we have to choose, even if there's power in what we never get to

possess—it's all precarity if we are honest with the truth and its serration:

how it's stuck like a knife in the bamboo cutting board

like a traveling threat that just hangs there

bothering me and my questions but better there than in my back.

(52)

I realized all this is bothering only me—there's nobody here to care about it.

Even if one knife wanted to cut me, the other wanted me to bleed out.

Let the years and years go. I'm trying to release myself from this kind of violence.

I'm not sure if it's melodrama or drama I am immersed in—

the truth often is uglier than it sounds.

What I will confess is that I am looking squarely at power in personal relationships to figure out how they also bleed out.

I have been thinking about what metaphorizing accomplishes.

Does it allow me to fling venom into the light and watch the vapor land quietly?

I will fling it like it has a target, but I am learning that targets are actually possessions that we treat in familial terms, and we must let them go.

I have accepted that I will not have biological children, and I tire of the meaning attached but respect my friends and relatives who have them.

I got pregnant way too late, after he was dead. Twice.

I was too old to start over. I mourned the loss of my attachments.

With any attachments, you are defined by them and have to pull them off like ticks.

When you are not defined by them you pine for them. Why? I will turn away from the pull to obsess over the ill-defining of myself by a gendered equation that, in the end, doesn't matter.

Doesn't matter, I must say. I will accept that my old life ended secretly, but in doing so, allowed me to be someone else who is still me.

Did you ever think that some of these problems, these powerful hurts, offer something freeing if you let them?

Because the way to erase someone's force, power, and hold is to allow their erasure of you to be the wisest instruction.

Didn't I learn this when I experienced my first racial epithet? In preschool. So early. I learn this upon reflection.

I look at the truths I was given. The hurt gives me up and with it, is hurt, and I used to live there, claiming it as suffering, but now I think of it as an isolated

world of what happened when that subject matter changed,

and you are here. Think of isolating the one word and unveiling its problem syntax for more

than you to bear. Then the suffering can become less mystifying, more just a dull pain, like the fractured ankle from fifteen years ago, or the wallowing

I did intermittently, which then becomes, what I learn is post-traumatic arthritis.

I thought I was in pain then and maybe I think I'm in pain now but I am not,
I am just thinking about what suffering thinks it is.

I thought losing all of them would be the end. But the end is an awakening
to look closely at who I thought I was. I am my end of the end.

Sit inside its life like it is the awakening that it conjures the knowing
inside of myself.

I can step outside of myself as the problem: this can earn me years and years
to step outside into a less weighted significance but a splendor nonetheless.

Maternal Endings

I'm not going to give myself away anymore,
dumped like melted plasticware calcifying across a table
makes my embarrassment pitch a hostile picture.
Prior to that I looked lovingly
out at a partially enclosed window
without a sill or view and it was boarded up.
I think you mocked my selfish gratitude,
and I was thinking we were closer than we were.
I keep looking at where that lost friend lives
because I keep distracting myself with a chiseled pain
that I let control me. I knew good and well, a long while
back, that we had vanished into a world of foggy spats.
Let it sit. Confront it. Notice it. Let it go.

When will I understand there are natural endings
and these are the human endings: all of them,
and friendship can fizzle if it's not kept well. I thought I tended
to our hearts, both of ours. And when I was vulnerable
I was still acceptable.

And now living in the precarity
is to both sleep and awaken to the truth,
to modulate in this consciousness so it doesn't scare.

Why do I hold on so tight when there is so little
energy in the world. Forgive me, I want to keep
saying this, but what kind of consciousness can I develop
to ground me in what I already have? I make a list
of the still life around me because it is still life too:
red gorilla grass, a lone magnolia that centers a square
and thus my being.

Why does my mind ache to tell her what I want her to know
that we both are suffering. She knows this. Everyone
suffering knows about the other suffering. They just can't help
you when so much hurts. So many people dead. So many people are dying.

Moment #1

I was not a centering line inside a brown canvas.
I was an atomic stripe of green grass in that time,
it had a sheerness which I mistook for opaque
because problems were heavy in the bust of shoulders
and not in the sag of a withdrawn shoulder-based head.

Notions were fresh but passed suddenly,
giving me up to a scent of what the past had been much
like its greenery and circumstances,
particularly, when I had no sense of my consciousness.

I know how to be inside of time, unearthing a quiet Sunday
passing more than twenty years to do such because
I wanted an earthen feel rather than unearthed time,
to ground the self to a footpath after feeling like
I learned what was important to know.

Because I am in that Irish cottage
from before remembering that my policy
of the past was a faint anxiety
lingering in small inclines of fret with trails
and traces like a contrail of wet thinking.
It was lush and had no centering line.

I can discern more accurately tone and perceptions

than I did in my prideful youth.

It was because of a then-sociality:

how I wasn't inebriated with attachment

but with hungry lust and pleas, and had a scent of its hold in my life,

but knew too much about addiction to let it churn out of control.

But did I even know what to write then?

I was desiring to write a novel.

I let him in for a decade and a half and he took all the novels out of me.

How easy it was in the past to start a painting

with the word moment,

and let all conditions be known.

How hard it is now to finish with it without it being permissible.

We sit in the cold wondering about all the moments

that were immomentous,

stricken with lonesome pathologies keeping the rooms silent.

When I see you understanding the lone line down the center of a small square,

I see how alive we can live in split-second circumstances

of this Irish minute

and last week in an English one,

at the Tate Modern with Barnett Newman on the wall,

only a little higher than your head and twice mine.

Onement

The lambent warmth of recollection.
It is brief but emotionally consequential.
Seventeen years ago, I took a job,
which showed me, over the years, pieces
of what a spectacular loss looks like against
the lucent light of lethal pain.
Here is where I held a remembering:
For her, for him, for them,
and then left it to pass from a large disparity
to a smaller one. This takes time and distance.
I returned to New York City and looked up onement
in Barnett Newman's Dictionary.
I realized that New York was no longer here.
I realized I was living for him,
who graced me with his partial feelings.
Ones I thought were unexpurgated,
honest, even if they were sometimes tepid.
But what truly held him was a glass of Pendleton,
an Ambien, or generic pharmaceuticals.
A bar where regulars honed their craft.
This skill was a replacement for what hurt.
In these afflictions and spots people could lie
to you and to themselves.
In art it is honorable, in life it is not.

All of this makes me see a nonesuch fragility,

and how a falsity grows holes

entrapped in gross figures of speech.

I try to put them back together

and my strongest self becomes my weakest.

I became a tumulted equation

in their grandstanding, stripped

of my own canvas. And gradually, you are

lost in gray, industrial weeds of paint.

Numbing the shifting spots of heartache.

I found a-tone-ment in a new oneness

I felt after he died and lingered in the sobering

daylight of my earned time:

from he who lost himself

and now I bear witness to his transparencies.

What is the committed treason they did?

Was it always first to themselves?

Before he looked upon my trust

he lost his personhood long ago.

Even as I picked it up for him, dusting off

the granules of a perceived irregularity.

It must have held up as a substance to me.

I did my best to return its radiance

to its proper owner. I had the one

to recover it. Now what I share is only my own.

Value in Failure

I need to write a poem about this feeling,
how when I linger in it while finding the right

word I am trapped within its possible
consequence of opacity,

some ashen grave set to permanently define.
Must I give you an image for you to see it, feel it?

Does it need a ring or clang or hollow yellow?
The sun's tableau? An ear to the ground?

What is the noise of melancholia?
Is it the sounding of longitude, of boredom boated like a fiend?

Especially when it finds the sea too close to
its teeth & mouth, and sets up an incredulous

relationship of creed and folly because both
differ in their incantations, their howls.

Just as feelings do when they persevere
filling the holes and circles and platitudes

in every word and notice, too,
the kill-space that conjures true-blue

sympathies that you must drop everything
to accommodate when it finds you hurt.

Long-Term Intimacy and Terminal Illness

There is a verity or a total manner that we slowly encourage
when we touch each other's skin. It's a soft pear with a winter bruise.

It's the place of world with two fruit trees in the splendor we created these
years, as one celestial body moves furtively and the other
carries it out kindly, recognizing the landed isolation is a body resisting obsoletion.

We become so grateful in the aftermath for any coupling we can muster
particularly when we accomplish release.

Your body is working so hard to endure these days
and my body feels the sad ache of new melancholia

for what is coming, for what is being taken away by fate,
and what of our hearts that become capacities of secular possession.

The Restoration

Not finding myself loyal to him anymore,

to what our life was, or to her silence, which begirded

me with its scrutiny. One released through death and the other by choice.

I can't roll the pain down a hill till it extinguishes itself

into the shape of its morbidity.

But now you and I—in the present moment—

strolling the streets of Claremont,

with their gleaming yellow and red-wine houses,

some of which might look like old-world Tuscany.

And in my whining, I stop, shuffle and want a solution

to all the estrangement you have no part in—

and have saved me from. I garble into my sleeve

with some ugly-crying: I need to talk about the past

and you want us to stay in the present moment.

Why do I lurch myself into the structures of emotional

hand-me-downs of collecting joyless encounters?

I had sufficient courage to let it go into its shending past along

with that toxic parental lust, genial attempts which turned

to beaten-up tracks of pleas. There was nothing left of me

in that world, you said, and that brought you to me.

I was in a subtenancy of sorts: with a non-family blank

with ardent vices: mimicry, silence, secrets, pills,

and thin ego-strength. I guess there was a thrill in forging

ahead with them by my side until it became a power play,

and I was a maternal beard for which they had unconscious contempt.
I don't know. I was inside one single layer of myself,
and still don't yet see how to take full tenancy
of my own singular existence, an olive tree—
twice removed—supplanted and toughened in heavenly
and bequeathing California, striped with its beseeching
rightly plains and cordial, din-musty mountains.

Living Room

My mornings in this living room
are writing verses while he sleeps
a little longer. He is a sparkling clear beacon
even through chemotherapy,
even as he grows thin.
He is still strong enough to guide us.

I don't want everything to go dark.

Right now, there are ups and downs,
and we are holding on to a life
remodeled now with cancer's precarity.

I didn't think this could happen twice:
I have poems about our life before
and now these ones that come after.

They have nostalgia that sits in the unbearable
plot of unknowing.

I'm a swirling stairwell of glass, waiting with the fat green parrots,
on the telephone lines while I fold laundry,
figuring in a bell of my shirt what I must do today.

But the overwhelm of sadness gets me.

What do choices look like without him?
These slanting bald trees

bury me in the futile thinking that
my grieving will be in the turn of their branches.

But for now I can be in a room that tells me I'm living in it.

You, a Graceful Place

I write you into a poem concerning my insecurities

titled with the chaos of what I find in your majestic dark roses,

you tenderly prune with a small jackknife.

Your discomfited smile frowns No in a serenity.

I just read a line, by the writer stating she had a "vulnerability hangover,"

which is what I currently feel with acute slants.

You don't know that you made my otherwise boring Tuesday full of sensorial ache,

and that my heart wanted to drink

its wine and get the sentimental out into the open field

with all the tangential attitudes that can adorn new feelings,

but this creates all aforementioned worry relating spurious need to "a face too real,"

as Robert Duncan would say. I see all the high-flowing rivers as wild

but singularly delicious perspectives where I feel the forehead lines

and styles of the face, of you thinking to yourself

and me finding the world real because I'm suddenly a stronger, more loving person.

Keeping Still

We hold an impossible diagnosis. It weighs on us
each sunbaked morning. I try to undo a certain sadness
because right now the chemo is working,
and we never know when it will stop and we worsen.
Sadness, I know, will turn into a unreconciled
and recontextualized despair.
Thus I am cataloging transitory emotions so I can
understand them better.
My mantra is to keep sadness and despair
as far apart as I can, in separate aisles,
on opposite sides of conjuring.
One can't let itself out but the other barrels
out the darkest blue without my realizing.

On Mondays our reprieve is a joint appointment with
Rachel, our acupuncturist, who ushers our limb-sprawl
on her paper-covered tables. We kick back, letting her cupping suck
our backs and needle-pricks (momentarily) sting.
A dividing wall that does not reach the ceiling
lets us listen to each other being treated.
We decide what ailments need tuning
and which ones our insurance will avow.
Insurance hasn't yet approved treatments

for his cancer diagnosis or chemotherapy side effects
but will approve codes for his shoulder pain
and my old ankle sprain.

We fall asleep in the middle of that hour during
a miniscule release to dream
out of our worry zones. We want it to
wander over to us in lightheaded waves.

I hear you churn a snore and wonder if I join you
in a hypnagogic sounding.
My head faces down in the cradle,
while we unconsciously create our chorus.
A cheering we do above our bodies crystallized
on the crisp paper sheet to an accompaniment
for our movement. Now a sort of liberty might transpire:
a soul and the docile body resting within unresting.
We accomplish this during acupuncture,
we find contentment that alludes diagnostics momentarily.

I Am Learning to Find the Horizons of Peace

During this second month of hospice, my love, where we don't know if we have

days, weeks, or months, we escape just an hour away to Laguna Niguel

whose beaches are a summer salve: an upper limb of the sun dubbing

a hue that evades the duress of our current reality.

I must try and see the whole of what's in front of me without squandering it.

I will write it out in colors and hues:

It is the dress of agreeable pastels we haven't begun to wear:

a stripe of salmon in the middle-sky, with rising periwinkle and silver-gray.

The sight of a pearling ocean contrasting the rust sunset.

The composition is habitually juxtaposed by drawing its own median lines—

descriptions for a worded freedom in a clarity the horizon affords.

This morning we gaze upon a marine layer hazing

above, dampening our room-air, giving you a worrisome sore

throat that thankfully disappears as we shift through the day.

I am learning that shifting through ailments, in particular,

is how to make peace with anything happening

at any moment, and that moving in and out of tricky comfort zones

is a kind of subtle reckoning with mortality.

Such as your foot stinging with numbness:

you are no longer able to put weight on one foot; or your needing

your nebulizer to open your chest in the middle of the night:

a humming of inhalation to release breath, to help ease pain.

We are learning how scrupulous

details or charted changes or quick problem-solving

invite us to new thinking: through it, I see your eyes alight,

a pure-blue sky of mapping after you've been enduring

some pain or challenge.

We work through the panic into insight.

I am learning this again and again.

We know that in Claremont, we sometimes can't see through

anything in our Southern California smog, but we have an interior

abundance of what we are learning. One must try to lose

all the anxieties in the face of the unknown, I try to think,

and not let it choke in the jostle of lying awake.

Today, I whisper I Love You when I catch your face in a stated vacancy,

or when you sit in a reposed silence looking out on the beach from our window.

I am writing your obituary on my phone, getting basic facts from you.

Where you were born and moved to. I don't know which views you had where.

There is first Milwaukee then Tacoma then Silverdale, with its view of

the Dyes Inlet to which you wanted to move back.

I know that part of the present moment was that we paid to have this hotel view

of the horizon but this will not be as eternal as what I now must forge before me:

the will to live without you and frame what you have given me,

that which feels immutable: The windows to expand into who we are inside

of our own, of how to make time an unmediated horizon

of catching, fabricated purples, of how to describe the wakefulness of it,

to the fact of acceptance and this holy blush of loss.

Vir Heroicus Sublimis

I praise the way you fall asleep in your car
when you are tucked into your garage.
The wood you hack for the fireplace,
in there, around you, like a blanket
of acres, of trees that make you feel
as whole as the car does; it's your
medication for your epilepsy
that makes you tired, so tired, like the o's
of your texts, like the sighs of your eyes
when they blink for twenty seconds.
I want to sleep in your car with you
in homage to the way sleep covers you
from the "fine" you say is you—
and you are a fine homage to your own
slumbering and what I find
to hold. I cover your scent with accolades
of the pine-scent I was carrying for another,
but I want to place it right
here between our seats because
you did carry me here.

Passions of the Void

that I've known | Is void indeed. | That I haven't | Is void indeed.
—Allama Prabhu, "Passions of the Void; 4" Vachanas

If I believe in a crafted delusion upon which my imagining conjures a will for onement then I am capable of avowing the void. What I learn from the *hall of experience* is that you are my *vine*

of desire. We *are* entwined in your spiral-bound notebook, which I found today with a list titled "Last Times." I think: Who disappeared, who entered the void, who carried us straight to it, and

then walked into the substance of the last time, a void. If I clutch the many "last times" I will stay in a bereft and isolated place. Is this also a void, or can it be a place of found meaning?

The grief book says that I need to dip in and out. I am full of nothing akin to onement, rather now it is a void full of suffocating ivy. Togetherness was a myth we had in earnest,

which builds a tractable way into provocation, into the gray sense of independence you offered me. But now, no candles, I will switch on battery-operated ones because I will forgetfully

walk away from anything lit. And yet, I will speak to you brazenly and in random fits with needy associations. My chatter that can only reach the docile you in dream-illusion.

An ornament is how we decorate the figure whom we've lost forever.

Abstract Expressionist

What is the textual equivalent of
a visual work? What feeling matches?
How to speak about suffering, art, and politics
when we live in vile times.
What is repelling me about building a
bucolic, representational image?

Abstraction helps me think about concrete things.

Can I write that I am
an abstruse definition that might be
justified in art, in poetry,
in music but not in my human symbolism?

In my waking life I feel indistinguishable
from all the hypothetical explanations
laid bare before us.

The earth is dying. People are lost in extreme rhetorical defenses.
The right wing is violent, amoral
and busting at their GOP seams.

Lone men wage war and shoot up communities
and I don't absolve them by calling them lone.

Bharatiya Janata Party, the ruling political party,
are committing violence in the name of scarcity.
We are still in the partition-land of 80 years ago.
Hindus against Muslims, committing violence
against castes. What can privileged castes do
outside of their ideas of commerce and when
does religion serve to buffer such rigidity?

How can I continue to bind myself
to theories, to blocking virulence in a liberal bubble?

And yet I want the philosophical interpretations
postulating unreal language, complex phrases, deep remarks,
ideal statements, to buttress the indefinite terms:
writing in a non-concrete voice full of recondite words.

What can happen in an ample transcendent announcement
with corresponding arguments encased in vagueness?

If I were in video, what would the true definition be
of my personal chrominance?

Will this presence give me tools to bludgeon with discourse?
Can I flee to the poetry world with my satchel of words?
Will it be transcendent to just connect our minds and bodies
and hope for the best? Is this a Vedic treaty?
Did it try to solve labor but didn't understand?
It introduced hierarchy: a world full of imperishable paint markings,

lines of personal goodwill and atrocity. What does our tremulous heart
build if numbers can speak collectively to this violence?

I don't want to retreat into art. I want poetry and art to revitalize
my energy to confront this unprecedented 20th-century life
of the Capitalocene as it's erasing us now in mileage
deep into the 21st century. I just question what
started with the industrial revolution
and the move from tribal to mercantile.

Again and again and again. It is abstracted and then real.

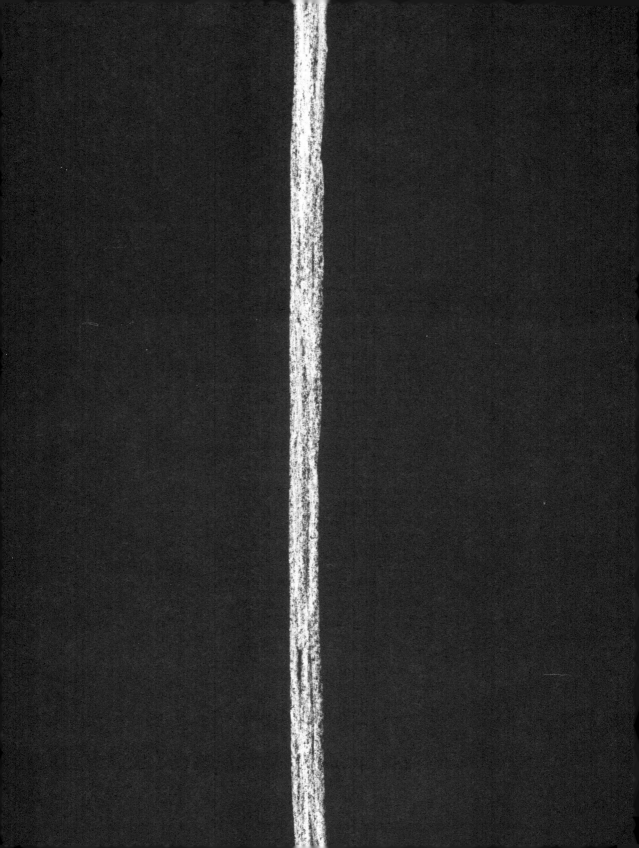

4112

ol IX. **oneiroscopist** (ọ-nī′rọ-skō-pist), n. [< *oneiro-scop-y* + *-ist*.] An interpreter of dreams.

of one- **oneiroscopy** (ọ-nī′rọ-skō-pi), n. [< Gr. ὄνειρος, a dream, + -σκοπία, < σκοπεῖν, view.] The art of interpreting dreams.

put **one-leaf** (wun′lēf), n. Same as *one-blade*.

(*Nares.*) **oneliness†**, n. An obsolete form of *onliness*.

onely†, a. and adv. An obsolete spelling of *only*.

ized, < **onement†**, n. [See *atonement*.] A condition of ne, + harmony and agreement; concord.

ut one
t capa- Ye witless gallants, I beshrew your hearts,
That set such discord 'twixt agreeing parts,
Which never can be set at *onement* more.
Bp. Hall, Satires, III. vii. 69.

for the
d with **oneness** (wun′nes), n. [< ME. *onnes*, < AS. *ān-nes*, *ānnys*, *ānes*, oneness, unity, agreement, sol-
ed fly- itude, < *ān*, one: see *one* and *-ness*.] 1. The
nded, quality of being just one, and neither more nor
nhed, less than one; unity; union.
inheit
.] 1. Our God is one, or rather very *Oneness*, and mere unity,
having nothing but itself in itself, and not consisting . . .
of many things. *Hooker*, Eccles. Polity, i. 2.

p. 451. An actual *oneness* produced by grace, corresponding to
the *Oneness* of the Father and the Son by nature.
Pusey, Eirenicon, p. 52.

p. 142. 2. Sameness; uniformity; identity.

e one- Fortunately for us, the laws and phenomena of nature
Unity; have such a *oneness* in their diversity.
nn.) *J. N. Lockyer*, Spect. Anal., p. 3.

a sin- **oner** (wun′èr), n. [Also written, more distinc-
tively, *one-er*; < *one* + *-er*¹.] One indeed; one
of the best; a person possessing some unique

on

print for *moneyer*.
that *oneyer* comes
(q. v.), does not see
only in Shakspere,
"an accountant of

With nobility and tr
oneyers, such as can ho

onfall (on′fâl), n.
aneval = G. *anfall*
an attack, onset; a
der *fall*, v.] 1. A
onset.—2. A fall o
of the evening.

onfang†, v. t. [M
fon, < AS. *onfōn* (
take, receive, endu
fōn, take: see *and-
dure*.

onfere†, adv. Sam
see, under *feer*¹).

onfon†, v. t. See o

onga-onga (ong′gä
A New Zealand ne
woody stem 6 or 8
painfully.

onglé (ȯṅ-glā′), a.
ongle, < L. *ungulus*,
having claws or ta
of prey: used only
ferent tincture fro

ongoing (on′gō″ing
advancing; progre

Index of Quotations, Aphorisms, and
Ideas That Have Guided These Poems

ONEMENT, BARNETT NEWMAN, AND GOETHE

"I must translate it differently
If I am truly illumined by the spirit."
—Goethe, *Faust*

Definition of "onement" from Barnett Newman's Dictionary in his archives, Barnett Newman Foundation

Goethe passage is from *Barnett Newman* (The Tate Gallery: 28th June–August 1972).

ONEMENT

(FAUST OPENS A BIBLE)

"It is written: In the beginning was the Word.
Here I am stuck at once. Who will help me on?
I am unable to grant the Word such merit,
I must translate it differently
If I am truly illumined by the spirit.
It was written: In the beginning was the Mind.
But why should my pen scour
So quickly ahead? Consider that first line well.
Is it the Mind that effects and creates all things?
It should read: In the beginning was the Power.
Yet, even as I am changing what I have writ,

(81)

The spirit prompts me, I see in a flash what I need,
And write: In the beginning was the Deed."
—Goethe, *Faust* (translated by Louis MacNeice)

HINDUISM & CASTE IDENTITY

"One is the outcome of the transcendent, and another is the outcome of the immanent."
—Isa Upanishad

"Revolutions can, and often have, begun with reading."
—Introduction to B. R. Ambedkar's *Annihilation of Caste* by Arundhati Roy

"One of the Strongest Fears Is the Fear of the Unknown"
—Inspired by Krishnamurti's *On Fear*

"The Hall of Experience" written after "Passions of the Void; 4": *God Is Dead, There Is No God: The Vachanas of Allama Prabhu*

Poem "Mothering." This quote comes from "The Holy "'Mother Who Is Not a Mother': Saradamani Chattopadhyay" essay by Narasingha P. Sil in the edited collection *Women and Asian Religions* by Zayn R. Kassam.

RACIAL CONSCIOUSNESS

"To the real question, How does it feel to be a problem? I answer seldom a word."
—W. E. B. Du Bois, *The Souls of Black Folk*

In the poem "What Is Sovereignty for the Hindu Today?" and with several other poems I am committed to thinking through Dalit Poetics and the decolonizing of Hinduism and Hindutva ideology that has been too pervasive in and outside of India today. It has led me to think about dismantling or reconstructing a Hindu rhetoric for myself and the construction of New Age thinking pervasive in wellness and consciousness-raising communities today.

Poem "A Moment Has Two Equal Parts and Many Decades." This quote comes from "Theosophy, Race, and the Study of Esotericism" by Julian Strube.

"Scholars such as Gauri Viswanathan, Mark Bevir, and Peter van der Veer have provided crucial insights into the political, social, and explicitly racial and colonial tensions and implications of and within Theosophy. Viswanathan has stressed that, within the Theosophical Society, 'relationships of power are never fully suspended, even as the occult appears to banish the distinctions that dissident Anglo-Indians so disdained in the colonial administration' (Viswanathan 2000, 3–4). Leading Theosophists were convinced that British colonization was necessary for the realization of universal brotherhood (van der Veer 2001, 64–65; Viswanathan 1998, 186–90). 'Westerners' and Indians might stem from the same 'Aryan family,' but that family was by no means free from hierarchies and power relations: it was dominated by the 'younger brothers' from the West (van der Veer)."

ORNAMENTATION & GRIEF

"Ornament" was written in conjunction with the Benton Museum of Art's "In Here: Solitude through the Benton Museum of Art at Pomona College."

"Ornament is never mere ornament. It is an add-on that allows us, retroactively, to fantasize about natural personhood." —Anne Anlin Cheng, *Ornamentalism*

"Orientalism is a critique, ornamentalism a theory of being. The latter for me, names the perihumanity of Asiatic femininity, a peculiar state of being produced of the fusion of 'thingliness' and 'personness.' As such, ornamantalism often describes a condition of subjective coercion, reduction, and discipline, but it can *also* provoke considerations of alternative modes of being and of action for subjects who have not been considered subjects, or subjects who have come to know themselves through objects ... It encapsulates a history of dehumanization, but it also speaks to a desire for objectness in the dream of the human." —Anne Anlin Cheng, *Ornamentalism*

"Art Is the Device to Get Out of Despair" is thinking about Antony Easthope and Sandra Soto's "Feel Lags (For José)"

"Grief is never straightforward. But there is something particularly disorienting when the person you find yourself missing is/was someone you were originally drawn to precisely because of their breathtaking aptitude for thinking and writing about the coordinates and texture of loss and sadness. Grief can assume a kind of doubling effect and temporal dizziness when laced with some dull awareness (or what José Esteban Muñoz might call 'flickering recognition') that your very attraction to or identification with the person whose absence you are now up against had / would have had / will have had / has something to do with the way that person worked at 'feeling down.' Harder still when the pierce of the loss carries the quiet and deafening undoing of an unspoken minoritarian solidarity. To be left behind." —Sandy Soto, "Feel Lags (For José)"

DEVOUT & FEARLESS WOMEN POETS

The poems of Lal Děd and Mirabai have helped me think about my relationship to devotional thinking, gender, and love, particularly these lines:

> "Resilience: to stand in the path of lightning.
> Resilience: to walk when darkness falls at noon.
> Resilience: to grind yourself fine in the turning mill.
> Resilience will come to you."
> —*I, Lalla: The Poems of Lal Děd*, translated by Ranjit Hoskote

MIRA'S COLORS

"*I'm dyed dark with him.* // I dressed up / put on ankle-bells / gave up on shame / danced // *I've taken on his deep hue.* // I took up with mystics / got called perverse / was faithful, true, in my body // *I'm colored with his colors.* // I sang night and day / described his qualities / escaped time, death, snakes // *His colors seep through me.* // The whole world would taste bitter / without him / it would all be useless // *I'm blue like my beloved.* // *Mira says*, O Mountain-lifter, listen / I'm drenched in your sweetness."
—Mirabai, translated by Chloe Martinez

Acknowledgments and More Notes
(As They Seem to Go Together)

Poems (in various versions) have appeared in the following:

"A Moment Has Two Equal Parts and Many Decades," "Inside the Sunlight of Lost Friendship, Squint So You Can See Yourself Again," "How a Tale Lost Its Ending," "Thinking Through Supremacy in Hinduism," and "Animal Family" in *American Poetry Review*

"Passions of the Void" and "Irresistible Contentment" in *The Atlantic*

"One of the Strongest Fears Is the Fear of the Unknown," *Chant de la Sirène*

"Hostilities That Are Not Hostilities," *The Chicago Review* online

"A Memory of Its Ceasing" and "Philip Glass" appeared in *Folder*

"A One Won" appeared in *Harp & Altar*

"Ornament" appeared in the Benton Museum of Art's *In Here: Conversations on Solitude* (2023)

"Secular Onement," "This Day," and "Friendment" appeared in *Mantis*

"Living Room," *MumberMag*

"What Is Sovereignty for the Hindu Today?" *Places*

"A Legacy," "The Imperishable and Perishable Family," and "Lateral Violence" first appeared in *Poem-a-Day* on *Poets.org*

"*Love, Death*, and *Shadows* (1959) in Missoula" first appeared on PoetryFoundation.org

"Abstract Expressionist" and "Elegance and Rights" in *Poetry Northwest*

"Metaphorically Charged" appeared in *Provincetown Arts*

"The Restoration" first appeared in *Water~Stone Review*

"Widowing" appeared in the *Yale Review*

This book is dedicated to thinking about caregiving, loss, loving people, and art; but also how one examines (or touches upon) anticipatory and deep, raw grief across personal and national crises: racial and religious hierarchies and oppression in times of duress and global nationalism. Furthermore, this book is for my mother and her vibrant devotional and spiritual path: She is Mirabai to me wherever she softly walks. Michael (Mike) (Hari), who, what can I say, was my deep love and moongazer, guided me through these poems to his afterlife. He healed me into them and left me to learn from them.

Poems here have been inspired by close readings (some mentioned above) of the Upanishads, the Bhagavad Gita, Vachanas, *Ornamentalism*, Anne Anlin Cheng, Goethe's *Faust*, Barnett Newman's Onement series, also found in a translation of *Faust* by Louis MacNiece, Arundhati Roy, reading the works of B. R. Ambedkar, Daya Pawar (see poem "Tree" from *Kondvada* and *Baluta*, his autobiography), *Dalit Text: Aesthetics and Politics Re-imagined*, edited by: Judith Misrahi-Barak, K. Satyanarayana, Nicole Thiara, *African American Poetry and Dalit Poetry*, Sudarshan Bhaware, *The Vulgarity of Caste: Dalits, Sexuality, and Humanity in Modern India* (*South Asia in Motion*) Shailaja Paik, Krishnamurti, Audre Lorde's *The Cancer Journals*, among other lines here as well as meaningful discussions about Hinduism with my father, Mahesh Sharma, and with translator, scholar, and poet Chloe Martinez, who helped me analyze and go deeper into my cultural heritage through her careful and mindful scholarship. Her translations of Mirabai (throughout this book) inspire my thinking of a poet-speaker who unsettles trouble and brings it to her own resilience. (I needed this thread of thinking more than anything else.) Thank you for the love and care: Teresa Carmody, Katie Kane, Katy Lederer, Colleen Rosenfeld, Valorie Thomas, and Maggie Zurawski whose respective senses of loyalty, logistic-problem-solving, resilience, and thoughtful discourse offered me the strength and joy of friendship beyond what I ever thought was possible during my time facing diagnoses, timelines, survivorship, caregiving, breakdowns, and grieving the terminal cancer and eventual loss of my husband, Michael Stussy.

I want to thank my family and friends: my father, Mahesh, my brother, Manu, my mother-in-law, Pat McCuish, dear friends at Pomona College, the University of Montana (& Missoula), and in Seattle who helped me in community and to find myself again (to find a onement I can live with now); poems were written at UCross, Yaddo, and MT/NY retreat, and with inspiration from the Barnett Newman Foundation and support from Pomona College and out of the care generously given by friends who

(86)

opened their hearts/houses/time for me during deep grief and growth. In particular, Vuahini Vara and Andrew Altschul, Vidhu Aggarwal, Rae Armantrout and Chuck Korkegian, Hannah Avalos, Brian Blanchfield and John Myers, Jordan Chesnut, Serena Chopra, Erishe Edwards, J. Finley and Toni Cook, Ahana Ganguly, Kari Gatzke and Michael O'Malley, Vicky Gray and Peter Bross, C. R. Grimmer and M. J. Castells, Stefania Heim and Peter Pihos, Woogee Bae and Corbin Louis, Catherine and Andrew Perez-Lopez, Hedya Klein & Klein-Horn family, Amy and Ashby Kinch, Ruth Ellen Kocher, Anna Moschovakis and Jonathan Lethem, Robb Hughes, Cherene Sherrard-Johnson and Amaud Johnson, Spider McKnight, Sarmeesha Reddy, Danzy Senna and Percival Everett, Kirsten Rue and Joshua Foman, Gabi Starr and John C. Harpole, Brooke Swaney, Kyla Wazana Tompkins, Divya Victor, Peggy Waller and Carol Ockman, and Dorothy Wang, and so many of my Montana and Pomona students whose kindness lifted, and many friends who took time to reach out (what an abundance!). And, Daniel Moore, much love & gratitude to you—what a brightness you returned me to in Seattle.

Heartfelt thanks to Joshua Beckman, Heidi Broadhead, Charlie Wright, and the Wave community for their literary anchoring, poetry-vision, and ongoing support.